Born into a large and very traditional Roman Catholic family in Forest Gate, London in 1950, classically educated at a strict Ursuline Convent School and City University, Carole Payne was an unusual and imaginative child. Her life was shaped by global events and chance encounters with interesting, and famous, characters. The swinging sixties scene, music, arts and youth revolution had a massive impact on her, as did her early first and only true love. She decided to write down her memories of this early life for her grandchildren and it turned into a bit of a saga. So this is *Part One – A Forest Gate Girl*, taking us up to her marriage in 1971. Part two continues her varied career and the adventures which never stop to the present day. Now with family scattered all over the world, as a grandmother with time on her hands, Carole Payne Berry lives and writes in deepest Wiltshire.

For Atlanta, as I promised, so that she can pass on the stories.

Carole Payne

TIMES OF MY LIFE: A FOREST GATE GIRL

PART ONE

AUSTIN MACAULEY PUBLISHERS™

LONDON • CAMBRIDGE • NEW YORK • SHARJAH

A CIP catalogue record for this title is available from the British Library.

ISBN 9781398416192 (Paperback)
ISBN 9781398416208 (ePub e-book)

www.austinmacauley.com

First Published (2021)
Austin Macauley Publishers Ltd
25 Canada Square
Canary Wharf
London
E14 5LQ

My special thanks to all the family who helped with research for this, especially the Woodhouses and the Paynes – the family trees are huge!

I must also acknowledge John at E7-NowandThen.org for his amazing blog and lovely photos of where I grew up, St Angela's Convent and Old Brownies' Association for pictures and memories, Atlanta for proof-reading and my husband, Chris for his patience with this magnum opus, forbearance when I struggled with technology putting everything together and encouragement when it was getting much bigger than expected!

Introduction

I've had a rather interesting time so far. I was a child of 1950, the half-century and lived through a huge amount of change in what has seemed a very short time. My mother always said she would write her life history for us and regaled us with many stories of her youth, but didn't leave a written record, so my recollections are limited. In the olden days before digital photography, we did have some treasured photos but over the years many of these have been lost. Films had to be bought, loaded into little boxes, pictures taken and the films sent off to be developed and printed. The best ones were mounted into actual physical albums but these are rare now. How precious these old pictures are now!

When my first grandchild Atlanta was born in 1999, I promised that I would write down the interesting bits of my life for her to go with some of the photographs.

When I was a little girl growing up in East London in the 1950s, most people had a Nana. Some had two – some, amazingly had more. They were matriarchs, founts of wisdom, allies in disputes with parents, peacemakers, strict disciplinarians and fantastic storytellers.

Now I'm a grandmother, I started to write my own story and quickly found I needed to go back much further than my own life to put it all into perspective. It was a daunting prospect and I put it aside to do in my later years! That time has arrived sooner than expected, the family has grown and my grandsons, Luke and Xavier and second granddaughter Isabella Rose, are part of the story too and deserve to know their rich family history. So this is for all of you, my wonderful children, Sarah, Siobhan and Dominic, my grandchildren now and to come, in my words. Some of my memories may not be quite what others remember, of course. I have discovered some previously unknown nuggets of information – and it's been a bit like the tv series "Who Do You Think You Are?" when I've delved deeper and deeper into the past. Like Forrest Gump, the life and times of each one of us in its course through history touches others and everyone has a story. Each "contact point" could be a story in its own right. It's been such an interesting journey.

1

Early Days in Forest Gate

I am the second of six children born to Yvonne and Gordon Payne. I was born in Forest Gate Hospital, London E7 on Wednesday, 17th May 1950.

Also on this exact date, the musical comedy film "Annie Get Your Gun" starring Betty Hutton and based on the 1946 stage musical of the same name premiered at Loew's State Theatre in New York City. I was to perform in this show 50 years later in Devizes, Wiltshire.

My parents were both born, brought up and educated in British India, "Anglo-Indians", I later discovered, of mainly mixed British European and some native blood, although my mother and other relatives vehemently denied this all her life, as if it was a terrible thing to have even the tiniest touch of mixed blood. I'm ashamed to recall that she scathingly referred to them as "anglobanglos", an extremely derogatory term then and indeed now. They were brought up at a time when being of mixed race was frowned upon from both sides, although they both came from wealthy families and had Indians as servants. All of their lives, I remember my parents and grandparents being completely pre-occupied with class and dismissive of any interbreeding.

Much of this has been referenced in books, great movies and tv dramas – The Raj Quartet, The Jewel in the Crown, Heat and Dust and more recently, The Last Viceroy and Beecham House. Once I started researching the family tree, my parents' and grandparents' attitude and opinions began to make sense.

The Woodhouses

Although I had no experience of what life was like so long ago in India, my mother and grandmother told us many stories of their own childhood, as well as stories their own "ayahs" (nurses) told them. These I half-remember in the sing-song tone of the Indian ayah, dream-like, sometimes frightening, full of strange words and expressions I never understood but remember phonetically! The memories are fascinating and precious to me now as I get older and don't want to forget completely.

My grandparents, Mary and Laurence Woodhouse

My mother led a carefree, privileged and happy young life. She was the eldest child, an only daughter and had two younger brothers. The three children were indulged and frequently got into mischief, especially teasing and playing tricks on their servants, who didn't dare to reprimand them. India was a dangerous place to grow up in, with the risk of disease and wild animals and medicine being pretty basic, but the children apparently had a terrific time. They lived in a large bungalow with many servants, a cook, dhobi (laundryman), punkah-wallahs (whose only task was to fan them and keep the house cool!), gardeners and ayahs for the children. They enjoyed their rather elevated position in life, entertained frequently and had a wide circle of friends.

GREAT-GREAT GRANDFATHER HEAD

Picture shows my Great-Great-Grandfather Head with his brother before he left England to fight in the Boer War 1899–1902

Nana Woodhouse's family came from Sudbury in Suffolk and Mary Elizabeth Head (her maiden name) was brought up to manage a large staff.

My grandfather Laurence Andrew Woodhouse was highly educated, a Latin scholar, worked on the development and management of the Indian Railway and was well-respected in the community. Mummy told us stories of him visiting the maharajah and going on elephant and tiger hunts. In one particularly ghastly tale, he was entertained at a formal dinner where a delicacy was served: monkey brains actually inside a monkey's head! Many years later, I saw this

14

portrayed in the movie Indiana Jones and the Temple of Doom, so I imagine it really did happen! I really hope he didn't eat it! In early photographs he looks quite dark-skinned, but my mother always insisted he had Scottish and Greek blood and I remember, as young children, wearing kilts of the Stewart tartan complete with kilt pins. My Great-Great Grandmother, Ellen Mary Woodhouse, was of Greek and French heritage according to the family tree and the surnames of Vaux and Albert (both French names) are featured. I have two large framed portraits of my maternal great-grandfathers (Woodhouse and Head) which they brought from India to hang in my grandmother's house.

Yvonne Moreen Woodhouse, aged 17

My mother was educated at a strict convent school, but hated it. She was not made to stay on after the age of 14 and social life in the form of balls and cocktail parties were much more suited to her taste and personality. She was vivacious and beautiful, knew all about the fashions of the day, popular music and local "club" gossip. She had a busy social life and particularly enjoyed the attentions of RAF officers and US military personnel. She was local jitterbug champion at the age of 16. Mummy was fascinated by the life of Queenie Thompson, 15 years older than her and later to be known as the great and glamorous film actress Merle Oberon, who was later to marry the film director Alexander Korda. She was of mixed race herself and consequently looked down upon by both British AND Indians, but was so fair-skinned and beautiful that she passed for a European. Several versions of her life story exist, each more lurid than the last, but her life sounded like a fairy tale. When her biography first came out, it was a great disappointment and sadness to find that her life had been pretty horrible and that when she came to England, she was so ashamed of her mixed blood that she pretended her half-Indian mother was her ayah and what was even more shocking was that her mother went along with it.

My mother knew my father from childhood and he always said he was going to marry her. She had other ideas and became engaged to a young British Army Officer she called "Dickie", whose family did not approve of the prospect of a "Eurasian girl" in the family. He was quickly posted back to Batley, Yorkshire and Mummy promptly married Daddy on 11th November 1947.

The picture shows (left to right) Uncle Mickey, Grandfather Woodhouse, Nana Woodhouse, Uncle Douglas, Auntie Cissy (Claire Payne), my Father and Mother, Uncle Rene Brunet, who later married Auntie Cissy, Uncle Guy (Payne), Nana Payne and Grandfather Payne.

My mother brought her exquisite watered silk wedding dress with her to England where it lay at the bottom of a cabin trunk for many years and was later used for dressing up clothes. It had covered buttoned cuffs and buttons all down the back. When I asked if I could wear it for my own wedding, sadly it was rust stained and damaged beyond repair.

The Paynes

My father was one of several children born to Vera and Walter Payne. There were two girls, Ivy (also known as Dolly) and Claire (Cissy). Being the older, Dolly looked after the youngest children and was much-loved. She got married young and left the family home, but died soon after of

Blackwater Fever (Malaria). I have fond memories of some of my Payne uncles, notably Uncle Paddy and Uncle Guy, who were nearest in age to my father, but I don't really remember the oldest, Uncle Ralph, or Uncle Douglas. Auntie Cissy was always a favourite.

Nana Payne was tiny and dark. I am constantly amazed that she had so many children! I remember Grandfather Payne as tall and well-built, with a shock of white hair and piercing blue eyes. My father Gordon (known as Jack) had lovely green eyes and was fair-haired as a baby, but his hair grew darker as he grew up, much like my son Dominic's.

Jean Baptiste 1726-1799

Walter Payne was allegedly descended from a European family of indigo planters. There was a Colonel Jean Baptiste of Bagnois, Beaujolais, in France and his ancestors were wealthy indigo planters from Europe. It has been difficult to find out much more about Jean Baptiste, except that he had a distinguished military career in the French army, fought against the English East India Company at one time, created detailed maps of the area and wrote on the history of the Moghul Empire. He retired to France and died in Bagnois.

My father was born in 1924 when they lived in a lovely house called The Hermitage, located in a village called Baguiati, in Dum Dum. Apparently, the village was named after early settlers. I wonder if this might have something to do with the town of Bagnois too? More research needed in Beaujolais, I think!

At the time of my father's birth, my grandfather, Walter Arnold Payne, was working for Martins Light Railways (a British Company) and accommodation was provided by the company. Walter was doing rather well and bought some land "up the road" where he built a beautiful house which was called Claire Cottage, in honour of my Aunt Cissy, their surviving daughter. This was in Jessore Road. Dum Dum is now part of the large sprawl of Kolkata and the fields are of course long gone. It's where Kolkata Airport is located.

The Paynes had a large estate in the north of the country.

My cousin Bert (Uncle Douglas's son) who has also researched the Payne family tree extensively, confirmed with Debrett's that the family had indeed settled in India from Europe late in the 18th century. Blue indigo dye was an extremely valuable commodity and trade with Europe had been long established over the centuries via the Silk Road to and from China.

My research uncovered a real and shameful fact. There was a notorious bloody revolt in Bengal in 1859 against the oppressive (and very rich) indigo planters: "Nil vidroha". The indigo planters "persuaded" the farmers to plant indigo instead of food crops. They provided loans, called dadon, at a very high interest. Once a farmer took such loans, he remained in debt for his whole life before passing it to his successors and so it went on down through the generations. The price paid by the planters to the farmers was meagre, only 2.5% of the market price. The farmers themselves could make no profit growing indigo and they needed to eat and feed their families. They were totally unprotected from the indigo planters, who resorted to mortgages or even destruction of their property if they were unwilling to obey them. Government rules at the time favoured the planters. By an act in 1833, the planters were granted a free hand in this appalling oppression. Even the Indian aristocracy (zamindars) sided with the planters. Under this severe and cruel regime, the farmers resorted to revolt. The Bengali middle classes supported the peasants wholeheartedly.

It was a terrible time of unrest. The revolt had a strong effect on the government, which immediately appointed the "Indigo Commission" in 1860. In the commission report, E. W. L. Tower noted that, "Not a chest of Indigo reached England without being stained with human blood." At the time, this was recorded in a powerful play, "Nil Darpan" (or "The Indigo Planting Mirror"). Excerpts from the play, translated from the original Bengali, were smuggled out of the country and the extent of the shocking and horrific exploitation of the Indian farmers was finally revealed to the whole of England. I have managed to find a copy of the play, which, in spite of its archaic language, makes a fascinating record of what was actually happening at the time.

My grandfather, Walter Arnold Payne as a young man

Walter Payne appears to have changed his name from Baptist (or Baptiste).

There was a family story that he may have been involved in a murder (unproven!) and he had to change his name to avoid imprisonment. My Father's brother, Uncle Paddy, provided a much less interesting reason: the name was changed in order to facilitate sending the boys to an English boarding school. Walter Payne's father was John Cecil Baptist, born in 1850 in Bankipore and his mother was Margaret Emily Payne. I discovered a quirky fact: they had six children who were all baptised on the same day in 1866, although they were born in 1848, 1850, 1852, 1853, 1855 and 1857 – I don't know if this was common practice at the time, but it does seem odd! Walter assumed the name Payne (from his mother) on 1st May 1923. My father was born in 1924.

As is common in many families, there was a scandal. Vera had another child, a girl called Mary, as the result of a liaison she had while Walter was away on business in Africa. She was "swiftly removed from the family" before her husband returned.

The Payne family, like many others in those days, had a tradition of sending the boys away to be educated and my father and his brothers all went to boarding school, St Thomas's in Calcutta (Kolkata), the best and oldest school in Bengal, founded in 1789. I didn't know until years later that he did very well at school, excelling at sports and mathematics and is named on the Board of Honour at St Thomas'. After they moved to England, he played hockey and cricket, which he adored with a passion, regularly for years. I never really understood (or appreciated) cricket, in spite of my father's enthusiasm and encouragement as I sat through hours of it at the Essex ground, completely bored unless I had a book. I did, however, share my father's love of boxing!

St Thomas' School, Calcutta

My father, Jack, far right, 1944 and next with hockey team, seated far left.

He was awarded several trophies for sports, notably Hockey and Cricket, which he brought with him to England and I remember seeing the silver cups proudly displayed in a glass cabinet. He also obtained a degree in Engineering, which I knew nothing about until the late 1990s, when my Auntie Cissy told me. He was modest, gentle, mild-mannered, devoted to his family and not at all ambitious for himself.

Gordon (Jack) Payne

Mr and Mrs Jack Payne 1947

My mother Eve (Yvonne Moreen) was the love of my father's life. He absolutely adored her and would do anything for her. They got married in November 1947. My sister Kristin was born in July 1948. It was a very long and difficult breech birth. The baby, presumed dead, was hooked out of my mother with an ancient medical instrument commonly used in those days (a horror story that haunted me while I was pregnant with my own first child) and thrown in a corner while doctors fought to save my mother's life. A nurse picked up the baby and realised she was still alive. She was a beautiful child with pale skin, black hair and green almond-shaped eyes like our father. She was swaddled (snugly wrapped in linen to keep her damaged joints straight), taken home and treasured as a gift from God, adored by her parents and grandparents and her devoted ayah, who would not leave her side and slept on the floor next to her cot to guard her from snakes and scorpions and other horrors.

Almost a year later, in the midst of terrible discontent and increasing violence and bloodshed in India following partition, along with many British families, the Woodhouse family, including my mother's parents and aunts and uncles, left India for a new life. They were all devastated to leave the privileged life they had known for generations, but my grandfather felt the times were far too dangerous for his British family to remain. My parents remembered awful riots and seeing slogans for "Quit India!" from as early as 1942 splashed over walls and their lovely homes raided and looted.

Quit India demonstration in Bangalore from Wikipedia
Picture by Dore Chakravarty ~commonswiki assumed (based on copyright claims)

29

A 2017 stamp sheet dedicated to the 75th anniversary of the Quit India Movement. It features the Martyrs Memorial Patna (bottom-left), Gandhi delivering his "Do or Die" speech on 8th August 1942 (3rd stamp) and a part of it: "The mantra is 'Do or Die'. We shall either free India or die in the attempt; we shall not live to see the perpetuation of our slavery." (1st stamp). Image copyright attributed to Government of India.

Quit India Movement Stampsheet

Some of the families went to Australia. My parents and my sister, then not even a year old, travelled to England aboard the SS Mooltan, a beautiful P&O vessel known as the "ship of a thousand romances" out of Bombay (Mumbai), leaving their heartbroken ayah weeping uncontrollably on the quayside. Mummy hated the long sea voyage, although the ship was luxurious and well appointed. She was sick much of the time and dreaded any sort of sea trip forever after.

SS Mooltan 1949

It must have been a massive shock to my parents to come to a cold, grey Tilbury after that long and depressing sea voyage in 1949. They had only been given time to pack one trunk each, so everything else in the house was left behind. Bank accounts and assets were frozen by the Indian government. We have never been able to recover our family property, in spite of huge efforts by my uncles and cousins.

My grandparents moved into a small terraced house in Chaucer Road, Forest Gate, East London, with their two younger sons, my Uncles Doug and Mickey and my mother, father and baby Kristin. There was a tiny galley kitchen with a stone sink and a gas stove, a coal cellar, a bunker in the garden which been used as a bomb shelter during the war and an outside toilet. There was no bathroom, so they took it in turns to use a tin bath in front of the coal fire. It must have been quite a squash, but they managed. Grandfather Woodhouse planted dahlias in the small garden which thrived under his care.

Everyone in those days had coal fires. The coal arrived by horse and cart in big black sacks and was tipped through the outside manhole into the cellar. I thought the coal was beautiful – big shiny chunks of it and to me as a small child the smell was delicious. Milk also came by horse and cart – hard to believe now it was over 70 years ago! My mother and grandmother shopped at the Home & Colonial Stores for our groceries. Everything was homecooked. Later a Sainsbury's appeared. You could buy a single egg and a single rasher of bacon and sweets were still rationed after the war.

My grandfather was appointed Station Master at Cannon Street tube station, which was quite respectable. It was a bit of a step-down from what he was used to, but he had his own cosy office on the platform, where we could visit him and have a cup of tea! My father got his very first job as a toolmaker with the Ford Motor Company in Dagenham, Essex, where he stayed until he retired due to ill-health in 1978.

2
1950

Forest Gate Maternity Hospital

I was born in May 1950, at Forest Gate Maternity Hospital. It was another painful breech delivery (poor Mummy!) and my mother said I was bound to be a dancer and singer, because I stepped out of her into the world, dramatic and yelling. I was completely different to my older sister with lighter hair and brown eyes like my mother. Unlike my sister, I had the Woodhouse features of freckles on my nose and rosy cheeks. I also inherited the Woodhouse temperament – wilful, stubborn and bossy. Mummy was very particular with how we dressed as little girls – always in matching outfits. Ladies wore hats and gloves and so did we. Older ladies wore furs, often fox furs with the heads on and glass eyes!

The only baby picture I have – 1951

One of my earliest memories is of sitting in my high pram (I must have been about 18 months old) with a large box in front of me. It was OMO – a powder detergent with a distinctive logo. It was used for everything – washing up dishes as well as for laundry, as was Sunlight Soap, bought in huge blocks.

Interesting logos which stuck in my mind!

Clothes and nappies (terry-towelling ones) were boiled and washed at home by hand, wrung out with a hand-operated wringer and hung outside on a line to dry. Our bedlinen, table linen and other washing went off to a laundry once a week and came back beautifully pressed with laundry tags attached.

We (and I assume all the other families at the time) received powdered milk and vitamins from the welfare department at Forest Gate Hospital. As a child accompanying my mother when she took the boys as babies, I remember it as something out of "Call the Midwife!" Babies were weighed in a kind of basket and the mothers seemed to treat the weekly sessions as a social occasion. From the conversations of the mothers, I learned about nappy rash and zinc ointment, cradle cap (sounds dreadful!) and the benefits of early vaccination for babies. Babies' weight seems to have been a bit of a competition. Bottle-fed babies were heavier and that was considered "bonny". Mothers received dried milk powder which had to be carefully measured out and made up into sterilised bottles for infants. We also had concentrated orange juice which had to be diluted with water, cod liver oil (ugh!), lovely rose hip syrup and a wonderful gooey malt extract and vitamin B product called Virol – that was delicious. With our growing family, it was quite a large order!

Our family doctor was Doctor Paul and his surgery was in Romford Road. He was very much like Doctor Patrick from the tv drama "Call the Midwife!" too. He was kind and gentle and lived over the surgery with his wife and young family. In his waiting room, there was a door in the wall which looked like a cupboard. It was the access to upstairs where the doctor's family lived and it wasn't unusual to see a small child clamber out from time to time! Dr Paul always had time for us, knew all the children by name and remained our family doctor for many years.

Me and Kristin 1952

Times became tough as the family realised now money had to be earned and jobs were not that easy to find. My mother took a part-time job for a very short time, leaving me as a young baby in the care of my grandmother. I was a good baby who slept well and while she was busy, I was left in my cot for long periods of time. I developed a lung infection and became very ill. Dr Paul got me through it, of course, but when I was older, my mother told me I had a "patch" on my lung. I never understood this and I have never had any health issues with my respiration, but I do have a small mark on my back over my lung!

My mother gave up work to look after us herself and grandmother got a job for the first time in her life. It must have been so demeaning to her. She worked hard, long hours in the Forest Gate Laundry, but I never once heard her complain. She still cooked, cleaned, knitted and made clothes for us and we adored her.

She was a brilliant cook too. I have kept some of her classic recipes written in her own hand. One of these was for her renowned Christmas Cake. She always made several, enough for the whole family and I helped her. It was a major operation, especially lining the tins with several layers of brown paper and buttered greaseproof paper. The mixture was made in a huge bowl and took both of my small hands (and hers) to stir. The smell was quite unique and to this day, we make it just as her recipe dictates, with butter, semolina, cherries and dried fruit soaked in Stone's Ginger Wine and Brandy, browned with caramel. We all had a final stir and made our Christmas wishes. As the designated 'assistant', I also had the privilege of licking the bowl!

Nana Woodhouse had two sisters, May and Antoinette (Attie), a brother John and we had several cousins. The little house was always full of visitors. Grandfather Woodhouse also had brothers – I remember Uncle Fred and even more cousins. I have been able to piece together a lot of our "lost" history from the extensive family trees compiled by these amazing cousins, now scattered all over the world.

Family tradition dictated that we were called by our second names, shortened to Molly (Kristin MaryAnne) and Betty (me, Carol Elizabeth). I complained that my sister had the more glamorous name, but Mummy insisted I was named after an actress, Carole Lombard. My birth certificate shows my name as Carol Elizabeth. As soon as I could, I added an e and changed the spelling of my second name to Elisabeth because I thought it sounded and looked more French. No one complained and it's been like that ever since!

3
1952

Queen Elizabeth ll was crowned in 1952 and we all attended a huge street party in celebration. We wore fancy dress costumes – Kristin was a ballerina and I was a little Dutch girl – I have no idea why, but our mother was very imaginative! We had cakes and jelly and ice-cream and waved union jacks. We were all presented with Coronation spoons and mugs. There was a real positive feeling that life was changing for everyone.

With our beloved grandparents

With some of the neighbours – Kris and I in matching outfits as usual with bows in our hair.

Uncle Mickey had joined the RAF, Uncle Doug got married and his wife, my Auntie Pat, was expecting a baby, so they lived upstairs at Chaucer Road. We all needed more space.

My father's parents helped us buy a larger house and we moved out of Chaucer Road to 1 Lancaster Road in 1955, opposite a wonderful park, which was to become my favourite place in the world during much of my childhood.

Early memories – a new house and burning my bottom!

In those days, we had no central heating and most people relied on heating one room at a time, often with paraffin heaters. As young children, we all used a chamber pot in our bedroom. This was dangerously near to the heater and I remember (painfully!) getting up from the pot and my brushed nylon nightie catching fire and sticking to my bottom. I went to hospital in an ambulance. I still have the scar to remind me and have been terrified of oil stoves ever since. The house had many rooms, a conservatory and a big cellar full of spiders – Kris and I told the younger ones it was haunted and they were never to go down there! Later it was whitewashed and we used it for storage and a playroom, but Gordon and Ian always believed the ghost stories.

St Antony's Church, Forest Gate

The lovely Catholic Church of St Antony of Padua was at the end of the road, adjacent to a Franciscan monastery and St Antony's Elementary School was right across the road from our house. The Franciscan brothers wore brown habits with sandals (and no socks) and had rosaries hanging from their belts. They also taught at the boys' secondary school next door, St Bonaventures.

St Antony's Elementary School

School badge

I started school in 1954, aged just four, but able to read and write, thanks to my father, who sat reading the paper every day with me on his lap, pointing out words as he read aloud.

I loved school from the first day. The school itself was an old stone building, the Infants School on the ground floor and the Junior School upstairs, with outside blocks of toilets and large coal fires in the classrooms – with fireguards! The classes were huge. In my last year at Junior School, there were 50 children on the register. Discipline was strict from the start. I was struck once on my hand with a ruler by Miss Smart for being bossy and that was in Infants School! My mother was horrified and I was traumatised. She smacked us at home with a rolled-up newspaper on our legs, but for someone else to do it was unthinkable. She complained to the school and I was given a sweetie. The shock was, however, enough to ensure I was never in trouble again.

In Junior School the Deputy Headmaster, Mr Aherne, kept his canes in a jar of linseed oil to keep them flexible – he was Irish and terrifying when he was in rage and Matilda's Miss Trunchball had nothing on him! The Headmaster was dear, gentle Mr Mangham. He read to our class everyday – proper, exciting books like *The 39 Steps* and the *Stories of Father Brown*. I adored him. (He was also Altar Server at the church and in 1971 he acted as Deacon at my wedding.)

I loved books. We were brought up on nursery rhymes and fairy tales, which I have passed on to my own children. I'm constantly surprised that so many young people today know so few. Mummy took me and Kristin and enrolled us at the local Forest Gate library. This was a surprise to us both – we so loved reading and this magical place was full of books! I vowed to read my way through every book in the children's section and started with traditional Fairy Tales, reading folk tales from other countries too, before moving quickly on to history and the classics and my special passion: Greek Mythology.

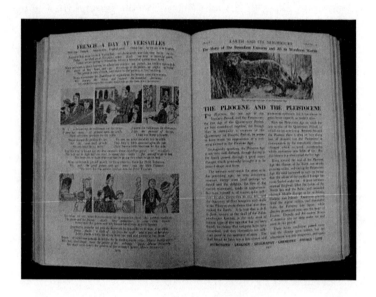

We soon discovered comics too – and what a revelation that was! We had The Beano and The Dandy. All the classics came in comic form too – the earliest graphic novels! The Three Musketeers, The Black Tulip, The Man in The Iron Mask, I loved them all. Later I discovered DC and Marvel comics and all the classic superheroes. There was a stall in Queens Road Market where we could exchange comics every week as well as buy second-hand ones. I learned grammar, spelling and punctuation from these unexpected sources.

Our grandparents invested in a set of Arthur Mee's Childrens Encyclopaedia for us. I read the beautiful books avidly – they were bound in red leather and had an amazing scent. The illustrations and photo-plates were covered in tissue paper, making them feel even more precious. I still remember a picture of waves on a beach and the quotation: "Forever the winds blow, forever the waters flow; not for one moment since creation have they been still".

I taught myself French, which was impressive to my mother when I was taken to see my Auntie Cissy (my father's sister Claire) and her French husband Uncle Rene, with my cousin Patrick, who was the same age as me, in France. Uncle Rene was in the French Military, and had been quite a hero during the war. He spoke several languages and was a brilliant interpreter. Auntie Cissy took it upon herself to teach me more vocabulary at each visit. We travelled by train and ferry. I loved it. It became a regular visit for me in the school holidays and my command of the language improved each time.

I taught my brother Gordon to read from these wonderful books too. I thought at one time I might like to become a teacher, probably because I liked being in charge, but struggled with my younger brother Ian, who found it all quite hilarious and just would not cooperate!

I also loved music, especially singing the hymns at morning assembly. I liked games, running and high jump. I was a good girl, tidy to the point of obsession, which infuriated my sister and brothers, well-behaved and obedient (at school, anyway).

My father was not a Catholic, but High Church of England and all of us were brought up in the faith and educated in Catholic schools. The church was the centre of our lives. My mother and grandmother were very devout. We all had medals pinned to our vests and said our prayers each night.

Every Sunday we attended morning mass and afternoon Benediction. Both services were sung in Latin and I loved them. I loved the beautiful church too, five of us were baptised and confirmed there and I returned years later to be married there.

The family grew. When I was five, my two younger brothers Gordon and Ian were born a year apart and I threw myself into my life at school. I was different from my older sister in every way, who, although very bright, pretty and sociable, was not particularly academic and hated sports, which I loved.

Flower girl (far left) with Kristin at the wedding of my beloved Uncle Mickey and Auntie Jean

Everyone had coal fires and chimneys. The chimney sweep came every year with a sooty bag of pipes which he pushed up the chimney with a brush at one end which eventually came out of the top of the chimney. It was quite fascinating to watch. The downside of this was the London smog. The air was full of foul-smelling smoke and fog – smog and infection. Although we only lived across the road from our school, we had little bags of camphor pinned to our vests in bad weather and wore handkerchiefs tied round our noses and mouths as soon as we were outside the house. By the time we reached school, the hankies were yellow and filthy with dust. Our hankies were also dipped in oil of eucalyptus to keep colds at bay – not sure if it worked, but the smell was lovely!

We used to all go once a week to the West Ham Public Baths in Romford Road. This was a treat as well as a necessity. You paid for a bathroom, soap and towels. My mother would take us all in together and shout through the door when we wanted more hot or cold water. The huge bath was filled and topped up as needed until we were all bathed. There was also a public swimming pool there and we had weekly lessons in the summer term from school. The water was so cold and I hated it. I never learned to swim at school. All the boys loved to jump in. I hated the splashing in my face and walking there and back (with wet hair).

Things must have improved for us by the time I was about nine, because a "geyser" was fitted in the upstairs bathroom so we had hot running water at home. We were still frugal about the hot water though and used the same bathful for all of us in turn, starting with the baby. It was no advantage being one of the older ones!

My mother staunchly retained her sense of superiority and protocol although we were not at all well-off. We had a live-in housekeeper called Flossie for a time. She was promptly sacked when it was discovered she had a gentleman caller stay in her room! We were not allowed to play with the other children in the street. It was considered "rough". We could have people back for tea, but I soon realised that "tea" was different in our house. Tea was after school for the children at 4 p.m. and consisted of tiny sandwiches, cakes and biscuits and tea or milk to drink. Any visitors joined us at the tea table. Dinner was in the evening with the whole family. When I had my own family, we maintained this tradition of a nursery tea.

1961 – Kris, Mummy and me with Gordon, Ian and Baby
Bernadette, dressed for a wedding outside No 1 Lancaster Road

There was a lovely lawn in the front of the house bordered by a splendid privet hedge, which was clipped regularly in the summer. I can still smell the blossom and hear the bees. There was a long-tiled path to the front door which was polished with Cardinal Red Tile Polish. One of my favourite tasks was to help polish it – sitting on an old pillowcase and being pulled up and down! It took all day but looked magnificent. The back garden was large, obviously cared-for in past times, with roses, a rockery and flowerbeds. My parents didn't have much time for the garden, so it became our playground until we were old enough to go to the Park across the road. I remember my cousin Geoffrey Payne (Uncle Ralph's son), as a young man much older than me, planting daffodil bulbs and explaining to me how they grew.

The Park (West Ham Park, previously the grounds of a large house owned by the philanthropic Fry family) was a magical place. We were allowed to go if we all crossed the main road together.

This was Upton Lane, a main road and a trolley-bus route. Trolley buses were introduced in the 1930s to replace London trams and try to reduce pollution. In those days, there was no pedestrian crossing. The nearest bus stop was after a bend in the road. The trolley buses were electric and very quiet, running on overhead cables, so while you couldn't hear the buses, you could see if one was coming when the cables were moving! They ran until 1962 – green vehicles more than 50 years ago.

West Ham Park itself was manned by a stern uniformed Park-Keeper we called "Parkie" and the gates were locked at dusk. As well as a children's' playground with swings, roundabout, see-saw and a hopscotch grid, it was laid out with lawns, tennis courts, a bandstand and a renowned botanical garden. All the trees and shrubs were labelled with their full botanical names and their place of origin. I learned them by heart and never forgot them. In my adult years, this would also be useful to me in my career!

In the summer holidays, there was daily entertainment for the children in the bandstand area – puppet shows, magicians, storytellers, dancers and singers – it was wonderful.

Upton House, the Lister house

Across the road, there was a beautiful big house, Upton House, the former home of the famous Dr Joseph Lister, who had pioneered antiseptic surgery. It was a vicarage by then and the lovely family who lived there used to invite us to come and play in the grounds.

Our elderly next-door neighbour, Mrs Scanlan, kept bees and we had a regular supply of honey. Next door but one lived a jolly Irish family, the Moriartys, with children of similar ages who attended our school and our church. Further on, there were the Buttons and around the corner, opposite the

Church, was St Anthony's Repository. This was a rather splendid name for a tiny corner shop selling sweets and ice-creams as well as stationery, holy pictures, rosaries, medals and prayerbooks. They also provided an excellent framing service for our church and school certificates.

We were not allowed to have pets, apart from a goldfish and a tortoise. One day the goldfish was found dead on the conservatory floor. It had been a very warm day and we believed Cleo had committed suicide by jumping out of the hot water in her bowl. Our tortoise had a P (for Payne) painted on its shell. We thought it was male and it was called Tortie – until one day we saw "her" digging a hole and laying eggs. They didn't hatch.

It was a very happy time, except for Skippy. We were all very nervous of dogs. Our mother told us of the time her brother, our Uncle Douglas, had been bitten by a rabid dog in India and had to have a series of very painful injections in his stomach. The harrowing tale had a lasting effect. Skippy was a little mongrel who lived further up the road on our way to Church. He was very boisterous and had a loud, yappy bark. We used to cross over the road before we reached his house to avoid meeting him. My younger brother Ian was particularly scared of him. One day, he started barking at the four of us while we were some way away and we decided to make a run for it. Big mistake. Ian, then the youngest, couldn't keep up and simply froze on the spot. Skippy took a chance and ran right up to him, probably just to play, but poor Ian fainted with fright. We thought he had died! The owner came out and picked Ian up and took him home. He was fine physically, but the psychological damage was done. He was forever terrified of dogs and so were we all.

How ironic that all those years in the future I was to marry a veterinary surgeon.

Although we were officially in London, we were on the edge of countryside. Wanstead Flats and Epping Forest were very near. The first live cows I ever saw were on the Flats and they were quite scary – if you ran, they ran after you!

Kris, me and Gordon with our grandparents at the fair.

In the summer, a fair arrived on Wanstead Flats. This was very special. We all went there by bus every year and enjoyed the sideshows and rides, candy floss and toffee apples. The smell of the fair was unique – one of those things that has stayed in my memory all these years, mixed as it was with the smell of the many cowpats on the field.

1957

When I was seven, I made my First Holy Communion. This was a very serious occasion and the preparations for it went on for months. We had to learn the Catechism by heart.

This was a small red book containing all the rules and doctrine of the Catholic faith. I remember the questions: "Who made me?" Answer: "God made me". "Why did God make me?". The answer was "God made me to know Him, love Him and serve Him and to be happy with Him in this world and forever in the next." I was a diligent scholar, but also very imaginative and kept myself awake many nights worrying about my first confession, which had to be made before I received communion for the first time – I had to be "in a state of grace" – what did that mean? We went into the confessional box at church one by one. It was slightly unnerving for a seven year old, speaking to the priest behind a screen. When it came to it, I was rather disappointed. I didn't have much to confess, so my "penance" was to say one Hail Mary – for a "venial sin", which wasn't very serious. Some of the boys were very proud to announce they had to say a whole rosary!

We were also instructed NOT to bite or chew the wafer of the Holy Eucharist when it was placed on our tongues. This was the consecrated body and blood of Our Lord and must always be treated with the utmost respect. If we bit it, it would bleed into our mouths and everyone would know what we had done. What a horrible thing to say to a child! We were all so anxious about it, we held the wafer carefully in our mouths until it dissolved – and looked very odd walking back to our pews with our mouths clammed shut and some of the boys trying so hard not to laugh!

First Holy Communion

The First Holy Communion was held traditionally in May, the month of Our Lady and was combined with a procession through the streets singing hymns to Mary which culminated in the crowning of The Queen of the May – a beautiful statue of Our Lady in the grotto of the church gardens. We all received holy pictures, more medals, a rosary and a certificate, treasured possessions which I still have.

The May Queen, traditionally chosen from one of the First Communicants, was the one honoured with the task of placing the garland of roses on the head of Our Lady. She was attended by six girls who all wore the same style of long white dress and held her train in the procession. I so wanted to be the May Queen! It wasn't to be. Jennifer Creet was chosen. She was a big heavy girl with a round red face and curly hair whose mother was head dinner lady at school. And she had an ugly name. Ah well, I was supposed to be in a state of grace and envy was one of the seven deadly sins, so I went along with it grudgingly and held her train. I had a moment of inner delight when Jennifer almost slipped climbing up into the grotto and placed the crown crookedly on Our Lady's head.

I remember there were several church processions on feast days during the year. We said prayers and sang hymns as we walked through the streets around the church. Being a predominantly Irish catholic neighbourhood, many houses displayed statues and shrines decorated with flowers and candles and people came out of their houses to watch. Everyone had holy pictures displayed in their homes – I still have my grandparents' much revered framed picture of the Sacred Heart – and containers of Holy Water were essential, as we were always blessed with holy water if we were ill.

My father's parents eventually came to live with us upstairs at 1 Lancaster Road. They were very formal and not at all like my mother's parents, who played with us and read to us. In their eyes, children were to be "seen and not heard". Every Sunday, my sister and I were beautifully dressed and taken upstairs to my grandparents to be formally inspected before going to Church. Nana Payne did always have a twinkle in her eye, though, and sometimes sang an old song to us – I remember "Two Little Girls in Blue". The upstairs of the house comprised five quite large rooms and a bathroom. Their bedroom was huge too, but crammed full of pieces they had somehow managed to bring with them from India – carved wooden boxes, large portraits in heavy frames, cabin trunks, beautiful dark furniture and a real tiger skin on the floor. It even had teeth! I never thought of any of this as unusual until I was much older. There were two beds in their bedroom where they received us. One was a massive wooden framed bed with rich heavy brocade covers. These were sometimes covered with sheets of newspaper, but I never knew why. The other bed was a single metal framed bed like a hospital bed with a thin mattress covered with plain linen. As was common at that time, a small paraffin stove stood in the centre of the room, although like most Victorian houses, there were fireplaces in all the rooms. The room smelled of Yardley's lavender water – my grandmother Payne's favourite scent.

Hilda's Pickles

Traditions from India were assiduously maintained, notably with food. There were a number of families who had arrived under similar circumstances, with little money but high standards and there was a sense of community, with regular social gatherings.

Hilda made pickles. She lived down the road from us and I often went to her house to collect a jar of something exotic. It was quite a cottage industry for her. The jars were lined up labelled on her kitchen table and the whole house smelled strongly of spices – pungent turmeric, ginger, coriander, tamarind. My mother's favourites were her home-made Masala Paste, Brinjal (Aubergine) Pickle and Saltfish Pickle, which I didn't appreciate at all at the time, but have grown to love as much as she did.

Mummy inherited some large deep cooking pans with lids from her mother which she called "dekshis" – I'm not sure of the spelling! I wondered much later on if this was also the origin of the word "dutchie" from the reggae song by Musical Youth "Pass the Dutchie" in 1982? These were perfect for cooking rice or curries for many people and were passed on to me.

There were other traditions too. I'm sure all families have their favourite sayings, but some we still use today are "sun and rain – a jackal's wedding", said when the sun is shining but it's raining and another when cutlery is dropped: a knife means a bitter disappointment, a spoon – money is coming, a fork – a visitor and so on.

There were also words that people outside of the family did not seem to understand. My parents were fond of using the word "galoot" to describe a lanky, clumsy person and "pilgarlic" for a stupid person. I have discovered that the latter is actually a word from Shakespearean times, derived from "peeled garlic", to describe a bald-headed man! Another favourite was "chingri" (prawn) for a small, irritating person – there were plenty of those! My cousin Patrick recalls that at school he used the word "almirah" in an essay, which was apparently unheard of in France and was told off for making it up. It was actually commonly used in our family and referred to a large and very beautiful chest of drawers, usually made from Indian mango wood. I still find myself using these words today!

As well as being very religious, the family was also very superstitious. In thunderstorms, mirrors were covered. Warding off the "evil eye" was very important and probably passed down from the ayahs. If someone looked particularly beautiful, they might put a black mark behind their ear! This was also probably partly religious superstition too – because of course, pride was a sin. If your right hand itched, money was coming. If it was your left hand, you were going to give money away. If your feet itched, you were going to travel. When going into a new house, a new bride must always put her right foot forward. And NEVER cut your nails on a Friday!

Cliff and his mother Dorothy

Cliff Richard (Harry Webb) had also arrived from Lucknow, India. His Aunt Olive was a friend of my mother's and when he visited, there was always quite a commotion, although I wasn't really aware of his celebrity status until I was a bit older.

He came to our house a few times and I had his autographed poster over my bed, but was much too young and shy to speak to him then! Years later, in the 1990s, I was working as an Events Manager in Windsor and he came to perform in a cabaret for British Airways. I made a point of introducing myself and he was absolutely charming and sweet. We had a lovely long chat about his Aunt and the old days!

Anglo-Indian Dances

In the 1950s and 60s There were dances ("socials") every month. It was a time for gossip (there was always plenty), live music – some really good bands and entertainers, dancing, Indian snacks and sweets and dressing up. Singer Gerry Dorsey (later to become Englebert Humperdinck) was a favourite. My mother was beautiful and always the centre of attention. And we loved to see her getting ready for a dance. It was a bit of a "coming out" thing for young girls too, as the boys lined the walls eying up the talent and the parents were just as watchful and ambitious as they considered suitable matches.

It was also a time for catching up on who had just arrived "off the boat", with news from those who had chosen to remain in India. It was indeed our parents' and grandparents' social life. Apart from the radio and doing the weekly "pools" (a kind of lottery) they had little else to occupy them.

Fun for the Children

On Saturday mornings with my sister Kristin in charge, all the children from five years old went off to Saturday Morning Pictures at the local cinema. It was my introduction to a lifelong love of films. One of my favourites was a film serial called "Four Winds Island" made by the Children's Film Foundation – about a schoolgirl's search for lost jewels. It was brilliant. How I'd love to see that again, but there are no surviving copies of it – I can still hear the theme song "Four Winds Isle"!

We were so lucky that there were two cinemas to choose from in Forest Gate.

The ABC was my favourite, because it was more of a club and we had a song: "The Minors of the ABC". (I can still sing it, if you like!)

There were popular serials such as The Lone Ranger, Superman or Batman, a feature film and something like Laurel & Hardy or The Crazy Gang and regular competitions. Being a very competitive family, we always entered en masse and often won – the Payne family was quite well-known! Sometimes there were even visits from guests like Chips Rafferty, who was a big Australian film star of the time.

Before decimalisation in 1971, our currency was pounds, shillings and pence. There were 20 shillings to the pound and 12 pennies to a shilling and there were coins for a crown (five shillings), half a crown, sixpence, threepence, a penny, halfpenny and farthings. We learned the value of money early on, playing "shops" with toy money. Five shillings (a crown) was an absolute fortune to us. Visiting aunts and uncles often gave us half a crown (two and sixpence) or a florin (two shillings) as a treat.

At the cinema, we had a shilling each: sixpence each to get in and sixpence each for sweets (we could get four blackjack or fruit salad chews for a penny) and we were there for three whole hours, so it was worth every penny to Mummy. If we had saved our money, we went to the Home-Made Sweet Shop in Green Street on the way home. The smell was heavenly and often the toffee was still warm. There were amazing sweets like rainbow fishes, spearmint pips, pineapple rock, fudge and liquorice. Tuppence (2p) bought two ounces of hundreds and thousands! Other favourites were sherbet lemons, bon-bons and of course, chocolate. Mummy would buy a large block of Cadbury's Dairy Milk chocolate and share it out. One delicious square could be made to last ages. Our Nana made special things like peanut brittle and coconut ice and occasionally puffed wheat (cereal) covered in chocolate.

We had a week's holiday with our grandparents in a chalet in Jaywick Sands, near Clacton-on-Sea in Essex, each year. We travelled by train from Liverpool Street station and that was the start of the holiday as we left London behind and watched the Essex countryside open out for us.

The chalet had bunk beds for us children, an outside toilet consisting of a bucket with a seat on it which my father had to empty and we thought it was an amazing adventure. Daddy finally taught me to swim properly in the freezing sea and we stayed on the pebbly beach for hours.

Happy holidays at Jaywick, Essex – me with Gordon, Kris, Ian and Daddy

We wore rubber swimming caps and knitted swimming costumes – they sagged terribly when wet! There was a small arcade with slot machines and an even smaller fair where we could amuse ourselves. We loved it.

Sometimes we went to Clacton which was much bigger and had a pier.

I was a very picky child when it came to food. We had eggs every morning for breakfast, usually "coddled" – very lightly boiled and with buttered toast cut up into little squares mixed into it. My own children also loved their "eggy-beggy" in the morning until one day, I learned that undercooked eggs could be dangerous! They have all survived anyway.

As a child I couldn't bear the smell of onions or garlic in anything. I didn't like many vegetables, fish or red meat. I suffered from what my mother called "bilious attacks", when I would be feeling sick and throwing up. I loved sweet, sugary things, which were not at all good for us and our teeth suffered. We had sugar in everything, from morning tea to bedtime milk. Our milk was delivered to the doorstep in bottles, of course. We had full-cream milk with a thick layer of golden cream on the top. My parents favoured "sterilised" milk in their tea too and that came in a different style of bottle. It also had a very long shelf-life in the days before fridges. We had condensed milk in cans which was already sweetened – so sickly now. A favourite pudding was tinned cream with a large spoonful of jam in it. Sugar sandwiches were a teatime treat. Once a week, the "Corona Man" arrived at our house. He delivered a case of soft drinks to the house for the children and the empty bottles were returned each week.

We had a school dentist who in those days just extracted milk teeth. It was an ordeal I recall to this day and ever since I've always hated going to the dentist. The rubbery smell of the gas mask and sickly gas and waking up feeling woozy with a mouthful of blood and minus a tooth like something out of a horror film. My own children were never going to have to go through that nightmare. On the plus side, we did get our teeth back to place under our pillows in the hope that the tooth fairy would leave a sixpence.

We didn't go out regularly for meals, but when we did, it was to the local Chinese restaurant as a special treat. We would have chicken chow mein and special fried rice and a small glass of coca-cola each – heaven! My mother would sometimes send out for Indian food – the earliest takeaway! – to the nearest Indian restaurant. Food would be served in our own container (or "dekshi") and brought home – very environmentally friendly. I didn't like spicy food then, but having the Woodhouse sweet tooth, I adored Indian sweets. They were actually far too sweet and a little went a very long way, but, oh! the jelabis! These were served in a thick orange sugar syrup too. Fish and chips was a rare treat and served in newspaper from the fish and chip shop.

We didn't have a television until I was almost 10 – and with all my books, comics and hobbies (collecting stamps, reading, sewing and knitting), I didn't miss it. If there was something special we wanted to see, we would go to our Auntie Ivy's house and crowd around her tiny tv set. In those days, there wasn't much on for children anyway and we had to be in bed by 8 pm. on week nights. The radio was always on and I used to sit for hours with my father listening to boxing commentaries – a treat for both of us, before we acquired a television set! We also loved the music radio programmes – Family Favourites and Billy Cotton's Band Show.

Aged 10 – Mummy had permed my straight hair with a "home perm"!

Early one evening in 1960, we were all watching Champion the Wonder Horse on our own tv and my sister Kristin took a tray upstairs to my grandparents as Mummy would cook for them. There was a shriek as she tore down the stairs crying that the house was on fire. Nana Payne had tried to move the paraffin stove while it was lit and the burning oil had spilt on the floor. Nana was beside herself trying to move my grandfather, who was more than twice her size and would not budge. He sat with a tight hold on a steel box and even my father couldn't move him. Later I discovered that his precious box held all the family papers. When the fire brigade arrived, the house was already well alight and they managed to carry him from the blaze. We all stood outside the house watching the flames and I can still hear the pistolcrack of the windows as they shattered in the heat. I've always been terrified of fire.

The upstairs of the house was a mess. The smell of the charred wood was unbearable. Our glass cabinet which held Daddy's sports trophies, family stuff (and my treasured ostrich egg) was destroyed. I was distraught. We had to move out of the house while it was repaired. We went back to stay with Nana Woodhouse and the grandparents went to stay with my father's brother, Uncle Paddy, in Harrow on the Hill. They never returned.

Grandfather Payne never recovered from the shock. He suffered a stroke and went into a nursing home. Nana Payne went to live with her only daughter, my beloved godmother, Auntie Cissy, in France.

It would be about four weeks before we could move back into our house. My parents told me that I could now have a room of my own and I chose the one that my grandparents had used as a dining room, overlooking the back garden. I could choose my own wallpaper – I chose yellow and lilac flowers and yellow paintwork. When the house was ready, we moved back in. My room became my sanctuary. Kristin also had her own room and the boys in bunk beds and baby Bernadette in her cot shared another.

Kristin loved being the eldest. She was a born leader and took charge of the younger ones. My siblings bored me and I often felt I was in the wrong family. Nothing I liked interested them much, except for Gordon, who shared my fascination with space, but he was much younger, so I just got on with life. I learned to knit, sew and embroider from my Nana and Auntie Attie and made clothes for little Berni. Later Nana left me her treadle sewing machine.

I continued to educate myself with the help of my beautiful encyclopaedias. The books were a revelation to me and I devoured them. I learned ballet positions and dance steps from the diagrams. I learned about insects and fossils, animals and plants, history and poetry and geography.

Although I was learning spoken French from my godmother, Auntie Cissy (my father's sister Claire), I had yet to learn any formal grammar. The encyclopaedia had given me the basics and I had more than a head start when I went to secondary school and started proper French lessons.

I also set myself the goal of teaching my brothers Gordon and Ian to read before they started school. Gordon was quick like me and picked it up easily.

Ian was much more difficult – a dreamer – and would not even try. Eventually I admitted defeat and gave up.

In junior school, I was now in a class of 50+ children. This was not unusual in those days, although Register took ages. We sat at ancient wooden desks with inkwells set into them. The ink had to be refilled every day. I became "ink monitor". The black ink had a distinct, oaky smell and you had to be careful with it, because it stained permanently if you spilled it. Yes – we even had pens with nibs that had to be dipped into inkwells! Our classrooms were huge and cold with enormous coal fires in the winter. The toilets were outside in the playground. They were cold and damp, of course and smelt of Jeyes Fluid on a good day.

We had free school milk every day at break-time, in 1/3-pint bottles that often had ice crystals in them in the winter. That first sip through a straw gave us serious brain freeze! We all had school dinners which cost a shilling (5p) a day. I loved them. I hated the hot spicy food my mother favoured, immediately preferring the plain "meat and two vegetables" and puddings with custard (bliss!) at school.

We had something called "Music and Movement" – a radio programme for schools which we listened to each week and I became obsessed with music and started to learn to play the recorder. I borrowed more books on ballet and opera from the library and learned about composers and choreography. I resolved to learn new words every day from the dictionary and started to practise them, both in writing and speaking, in school. I nagged my parents mercilessly and we got a piano! I started lessons with Mr Bebb.

After the initial elation, reality set in. Mr Bebb was boring so the lessons were boring. The incessant exercises were boring and the room I had to practise in was cold most of the time and my toes went numb. I so wanted to learn, but my Ezra Read book of piano exercises made it really tedious and dull. In those days, we kept one room for "special" and that was the "hall-room" in our house – the room where the piano was kept and where we entertained formally. I was very surprised to discover that my mother had a real talent for playing by ear – and I was shocked that I could not. Even today, I still have to have sheet music in front of me. My love of all kinds of music remains with me to this day.

What I did discover was that I loved to sing and act (and, being bossy from the start, especially to direct!). We were encouraged to "perform" a party piece at Christmas for grandparents and visiting aunties, uncles and cousins. My earliest recollection of this was singing "Kiss Me, Honey, Honey, Kiss Me", a Shirley Bassey hit from 1957! I must have seen her perform it, because I remember doing her hands and weird facial expressions – and the audience was very appreciative, so I knew I'd got it right! My sister Kristin looked better, though, so this became "her" party piece, while I did the rather less spectacular, but more melodic, "Tammy" as Debbie Reynolds, my real favourite. We were also rather good at "Sisters"!

I loved music, all kinds. My grandparents had an ancient gramophone with real records – big thick shiny black discs – which were played with a pin scratching on the surface. There was even a little tin box of pins! Their record collection of "78s" was amazing. 78 rpm meant 78 revolutions of the record per minute, which was the speed at which they were played. The records were kept in brown paper sleeves to protect them from scratches and dirt. The music was a mixture of popular classics, lots of operatic arias and famous choruses, jazz and music hall. My grandfather also played the mouthorgan rather well. He entertained us hugely with comic songs which we heard on Children's Favourites on the radio – our own favourites were Susanna's a Funniful Man, Abdul the Bulbul, Sparky's Magic Piano and the Three Billy Goats Gruff.

My parents were more modern: we had a record player in a cabinet which played 78s AND 45s AND 33 1/3s!! 45s were usually double-sided singles and 78s and 33 1/3 were Extended Play (EPs) albums of songs. We had albums of Elvis Presley, Frank Sinatra and Fats Domino (Jazz), Jim Reeves (Country and Western), musicals (my favourites) and singles of all sorts, including classical music. Daddy's favourite song was Don't Fence Me In. Mummy loved all the jazzy songs and dance numbers, Fats Domino as well as Sinatra and, of course, Elvis Presley.

We entertained a lot and had regular parties. Children's parties usually included grandparents and all the aunties and uncles as well as cousins and schoolfriends. On the Woodhouse side, I remember in particular Uncle Doug and Auntie Pat with Lynn and Jill (the youngest, John, wasn't yet born) and the twins Aggie and Eleanor with Great Auntie May, who lived in Bexley Heath, Uncle Mickey and Auntie Jean before they went to live in Canada and Great Uncle Fred and Great Uncle John. Nana Woodhouse was the centre of all family gatherings. Later, my mother took over as the matriarch. On the Payne side Auntie Janet and Uncle Paddy brought Michelle and Jonathan, Uncle Guy with his children (with whom I have recently re-connected), Auntie Cissy and Uncle Rene with Patrick, cousin Bert and many more whose names I don't recall.

1958 The Biros

A lovely Hungarian family called Biro suddenly came to stay with us. All we were told was that they had been forced to leave their country suddenly and had nothing and nowhere to live. Later I read that 200,000 refugees had left Hungary in the wake of the Hungarian Revolution of 1956. Josef and Magda had two little boys about the same ages as me and Kris. The family all remained good friends with our parents for many years.

One day Josef came back to visit us and mummy served him mulligatawny soup in a cup. He had obviously expected it to be tea, because he put sugar in it! Mummy laughed and was going to throw it away, but he refused and said he would drink it anyway because he remembered so well how it felt to

73

go hungry and could not bear to waste food. The incident still moves me to this day. I was so shocked and cried when he told of how he and Magda had to swim across a river to escape, each of them with one of the boys holding on tightly to them.

4

The Space Thing – 1959

When I was eight or nine, I became fascinated with space. I think I must have picked up on the "Space Race" around 1959. I read everything I could find about the planets and the stars and as much science fiction I could pick up from the local library too.

My imagination was fuelled by the snippets of news I heard on the radio. I also began to collect stamps and it became a bit of an obsession.

Astronauts John Glenn and Yuri Gagarin featured on stamps from the US and Russia. I had to have them. I wrote letters to both John F Kennedy and Nikita S Kruschev to ask for stamps.

To my surprise and delight, they replied – personal letters to me with stamps and even an invitation from Mr Kruschev himself to join the Children's Soviet Party! My mother was terrified that I would be converted to Communism! I continued to collect stamps for years afterwards.

Stamp collecting became a bit of an obsession too. Mummy later worked part time at the GPO (Sorting Office) and I had quite an extensive collection of First Day Covers.

I kept the letters and stamps right up until I got married in 1971, when I discovered that my mother had had a clear out and they were lost, along with my cherished autograph books. I was heartbroken, but at least I had the memories, which my brother Gordon shared as he too was caught up in the excitement of the time.

Christmas Traditions

Christmas was massively important in our family. As we attended church so regularly, our lives were ruled to a large extent by the church calendar. Once Advent started, so too did the excitement and anticipation of Christmas. There was the annual visit to Father Christmas at Boardmans department store or the Co-op in Stratford. These were often quite extravagant theatrical productions, always involving a moving something – maybe a rocket or a train, to see Father Christmas himself and get a present. There was a pantomime at some point and for me the chance to be the lucky child invited onto the stage – I always had to be there!

Daddy went to Smithfield Market in London to collect a fresh turkey on Christmas Eve. Mummy always made the stuffing the day before with vegetables and sausage meat. Then the turkey was cooked, sometimes overnight, so we woke up to the smell of it.

We had a huge Christmas tree, with the same ornaments carefully kept over the years. The baubles were exquisite, precious, made of glass and bought from Selfridges. At least one shattered each year and had to be replaced. The children made paper chains to hang around the house and holly and mistletoe went up on Christmas Eve. We still have the little

Father Christmas in his sleigh pulled by his reindeer. This travels up the tree from the bottom to the top magically every year.

Like children the world over, we woke up as soon as Father Christmas had left our presents. These would be in stockings at the end of our beds, a small toy or two, a book, usually an "Annual", a game or a jigsaw puzzle, with an apple, an orange and some nuts tucked in the bottom. This was long before shop made pre-filled stockings. Larger presents would be placed on the bed.

Paper dress-up dolls

I remember my favourite presents – a toy piano, a card dressing up doll with paper outfits you cut out from books and hung onto the doll, a Sweet Shop with tiny bottles of sweeties and a cash register, a Post Office with play stamps and stationery, a child's sewing machine that sewed in chainstitch!

One year I had wished for a bride doll. When I woke up, I saw my sister and I both had dolls, mine a bride doll in a beautiful white dress and veil, but to my horror it was a bisque china doll, so her head was hard and dark and it didn't go with her blonde hair! I cried for days because I wanted my sister's, which was more modern (plastic), pale with lovely short curly hair. Such an ungrateful child! Another year I had wished for a Cinderella watch made by Timex – they came in their own glass slipper. I opened my present and found not a glass slipper but a wonderful clockwork Cinderella figure that waltzed – and the watch itself on its pretty blue strap – I was so thrilled with it! Our parents didn't have much money to spare, but they did spoil us at Christmas. The boys had Meccano construction sets or model aeroplanes which I also loved and played with whenever I could. With all our presents from family and friends we were very lucky indeed. Our parents were very generous too. There was a local family with two girls the same age as me and Kris who were not at all well off and didn't receive any presents. Mummy asked us to choose one present each from ours to give them. I reluctantly chose to give up my lovely little toy cooker and Kris chose a book so they would have something each.

We went to church early (communion had to be taken on an empty stomach) and came back to eat breakfast which was fried eggs, ham and stuffing.

Christmas Dinner was usually at Nana's house. We all gathered for VP Wine (an English fortified wine, still available), eggnog (a peculiar concoction made with eggs, nutmeg, sugar and brandy) or Stone's Ginger Wine and cake and orange squash for the children. Nana cooked a traditional Indian meal for the grown-ups which they ate downstairs. Upstairs, my darling Auntie Pat cooked a delicious roast chicken dinner, jelly and ice-cream for the children. It was wonderful.

Bullying (or Racism?) 1960

I only once encountered any kind of racism and I didn't really understand what that was all about at the time. I was about 10 and visiting my grandparents at their house in Chaucer Road, about a quarter of a mile away. I remember it was a hot summer's day. As I walked along, I became aware of a group of young boys I'd seen hanging around before but didn't know. They started to follow me and jeered at my tanned skin and hair, which was in plaits and sort of stripy, as it has always been streaked with blonde, especially when I'd been in the sun. They started to call out something about "red Indians" and pull at my plaits. I got a bit scared and tried to run, but they gathered round me laughing and backed me up against the wall. The leader, an older boy of about 12 or 13, took out a penknife. I was terrified. He said he was going to skin me to see if I was as brown under my skin. I think the others must have been as scared and shocked as I, because they released their hold on me and I ran as fast as I could to my Nana's house.

I was in a dreadful state and the Police were called. They found the boys and had a word with them. No charges were made as I was physically unharmed. I just wonder how that would go down these days!

5

The Sixties

1961 A Convent Girl

My sister had been sent to St Angela's Convent School at the age of 11 and I was to follow her. This was a prestigious Ursuline convent about a mile from our house. About the same time, the 11-plus examination was being reviewed and was being replaced by an intelligence test. My primary school put us all through both tests! When the results were announced, I had received the second highest marks in Greater London. My last school report before secondary school showed me in joint 1st place in a class of 50 children.

I achieved 99 out of 100 in spelling, which deeply annoyed me, as the only word I got wrong was "hydraulic", because it was pronounced "hydrolic"! My rival in the subject, Martin Donohoe, also got it wrong for the same reason, but it was no consolation.

St Angela's Convent

St Angela's was divided into two parts, grammar and technical, named Brescia and Merici (after St Angela Merici, who founded the Ursuline order). Applicants had to take a further test to see which part they would be allocated to. I was sent to Brescia, the grammar section. My sister Kristin was already in Merici, the technical and secretarial section. There was strict segregation, even for siblings, so we didn't mix at all at school. We had little in common academically and this lasted all our lives, although Kris was bright and did well in her secretarial exams and later became a teacher! Her daughter, Beth, has a Master's Degree in International Education and is a teacher too, while her son, Alex, is a published writer.

I thought the school uniform was fantastic. There was only one supplier, Boardmans department store in Stratford and we had to make an appointment to be measured up and order it.

Boardmans Price List!

So exciting. I had no idea how expensive it must have been for our parents at the time, but we had to have it all, although the summer dresses could be made more cheaply from the shop pattern. There was a summer and winter uniform.

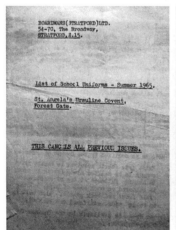
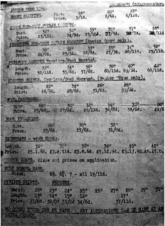

From wearing a bottle green gymslip and blazer at St Antony's, it changed to "nigger" brown. In those days, this was not a bad word, merely a common description of the very dark brown colour. In 1961, the gymslip was pleated with a square yoke, worn with a white shirt and brown and yellow tie. In my fifth year, this changed to a cream blouse and pleated brown skirt – much more modern! There was a brown gabardine full-length coat, brown and yellow scarf, brown felt hat and a brown beret. Berets had to be worn outside at all times. Hair had to be tidy – mine was usually in plaits. And "Brownies", as we now were called, were never, ever, to be seen eating outside in our uniforms, or face "report" by a prefect. Juniors had to wear white ankle socks; stockings were only worn by sixth-formers. The summer uniform was a turquoise and white shirt-waister dress with a brown cardigan and a very smart brown blazer with gold trim. House badges were pinned on and merit badges had to be stitched on. The school motto was "Serviam" which means "I will serve" in Latin. This was the cry of St Michael the Archangel as a response to Lucifer's "I will not serve" when God put the angels to the test. I still have my enamel Serviam badge.. We even had to have "nigger brown" thick cotton knickers! For PE, we wore brown divided skirts with long socks. The rules were very strict. The hem of the gym shorts had to touch the ground when you knelt down – definitely no short shorts! There was a rule book about dress and behaviour too. I remember watching horrified as a nun painfully combed out one girl's (then very fashionable) beehive hairdo!

Serviam Badge

My school banner

From the first moment I stepped into the convent, I adored it. The smell of the lavender and beeswax polish, the cool silence of the chapel and the library, the discipline, the sense of timelessness and tradition entranced me. There were Honours Boards with the names of past pupils inscribed in gold. The famous Shakespearean actress Margaret Tyzack's name was there! The nuns wore full black habits, with starched white wimples and collars. They looked so uncomfortable and hot. But they seemed to glide around the place and spoke in soft voices. The days were ruled by bells and punctuated by prayers.

Having come from a final mixed class of 50 in my primary school, I was both shocked and delighted to find I was now in one of only 26 girls – and they were all like me! We were put into houses named after the great royal houses. I was in Norman and our house colour was yellow (my favourite). We were again divided into classes based upon our performance in the entrance examinations. These were Wiseman, Manning and Newman (named after English Cardinals). I was in Wiseman. I used to have a regular weekly comic at the time called Bunty. In it was a story called "The Four Marys" – four girls who all went to a school just like mine and had adventures.

The Four Mary's Bunty

We had several Marys in my class too, every day was an adventure and I was in my element!

1962 was the centenary of the school's founding and Mother Peter, our inspirational Geography teacher, instigated a brilliant project for us to mark it. We made maps of Forest Gate from 100 years before and compared life to modern times. I found it all fascinating. Forest Gate was such an interesting place, dating from Anglo-Saxon times! We discovered that the first known record of the name "Forest Gate" comes from parish registers of the late 17th century and describes a gate placed across the modern Woodford Road to prevent cattle straying from the open area of Wanstead Flats (borders of Epping Forest) onto the main Roman road (now Romford Road) which linked the ancient roman town of

Camulodonum (Colchester) to Londinium (London). The gate itself was located close to the former Eagle & Child public house. It never was a toll gate and was demolished along with the keepers' cottage in 1881. The lovely old pub, The Spotted Dog, near my grandparents' house, was originally a hunting lodge for King Henry VIII.

Schooldays at St Angela's started with morning assembly at 8:50 a.m., when we all marched into the Hall to piano music. I loved the structure. The day was marked by bells and prayers. Lessons went on until 12 noon, when the bell for the Angelus was rung. Lunch was taken in the big Dining Hall, then new, at tables of 8, with Grace said before and after meals. Running anywhere inside, apart from in Games, was strictly forbidden. Games was compulsory and we had tennis courts and netball courts as well as fields to run in. In bad weather, we used the gym for "Pirates" to let off excess energy.

Every month we had "degrees". This was the tracking measurement adopted by the school and again, we all marched in by class to music. Our names were called out according to our average marks in each subject for that month and we had lines to stand on – A, B and C etc. Anyone getting a D or E more than twice was moved down to the next class. Similarly, any girl who merited straight As for a term went up a class. I was lucky and stayed in Wiseman throughout my school career. Our report books were sent home to our parents each month to be checked and signed, so everyone knew exactly how they were doing. Once a year we had Prizegiving – a very, very special event. I still have the two prizes I was awarded, both for Latin, once in my 3rd year and again in my final year. One was Thomas Hardy's *The Woodlanders* and the other a volume of Shelley's poetry – both favourite writers of mine.

We also had something called "Third Degree", which was terrifying. This was the worst form of discipline and everyone dreaded it. It was meted out to any Brownie who had seriously broken the rules, for example, for cheating in an exam. I only saw this once in my school career. Reverend Mother stood on the stage at a desk with a bell and a large book, reminiscent of the "bell, book and candle" of the catholic church, a ceremony used to excommunicate anyone who had committed a particularly grievous sin. This time there was no piano music, just an eerie and foreboding silence and the whole school assembled in the Hall. The miscreant's name was called, the bell rung and she had to walk up the steps to the desk and write her name in the book. Humiliated, she then had to turn and walk all the way back. It was horrible to watch and the psychological torture far worse than any corporal punishment.

The School magazine was called "The Uptonian". It was quite an honour to have anything printed in it and we all submitted items each year, hoping to be selected. Back issues were stored in the school library, but a fire some years ago destroyed them. Luckily, some of the old brownies kept their copies and two have been sent to me. In one, my essay on Life in the Future was published, written when I was in my second year at school. I was thrilled.

I was always an eccentric, if imaginative child!

Each May we celebrated Founder's Day. We all wore marguerites, large white daisies and enjoyed the May Fayre and picnic on the field and sang the school song – I still know all the words. And it was always a sunny day. The school still celebrates in the same way – many years later I took my daughter Sarah and then baby granddaughter Atlanta to share the memory.

The school day finished at 4 p.m., but I often stayed on in school for an hour or more doing my prep, because home was too crowded and noisy. This guaranteed I got all my homework done on time and I was a high achiever.

My favourite subjects were English, French, Latin and Music – all of which were indulged in Drama, which I adored, although I was self-conscious about my lisp, so was reluctant to put myself forward. This changed as I got older and grew more confident! The drama teacher, Miss Connolly, was a paragon. She was tall, willowy with white hair and striking blue eyes and wore the most outlandish clothes – such a contrast to the plain black Ursuline habit of the nuns, or the academic gowns the other lay teachers wore. We did a lot of work on personal presentation, deportment and public speaking, all of which have come in useful in my adult life!

The school productions were always outstanding and I loved them – everything from farce and Shakespeare to musicals and some amazing classical pieces – Menotti's Amahl and the Night Visitors and Britten's Noyes Fludde. Choir was also fantastic and we entered festivals every year. We took part in Britten's Ceremony of Carols and performed this with other school choirs at the Royal Festival Hall. Our music teacher arranged for us to have free tickets for regular Saturday afternoon performances at the Festival Hall where we could sit behind the percussion. It was a bit noisy, but great fun and it meant we had a unique experience of live orchestras whenever we wanted.

In English we studied and performed two Shakespeare plays each year and I developed a lifelong passion for William Shakespeare. I also discovered a rare gift – I could remember whole chunks of the text by making a kind of photographic image of the printed page in my head. This was maximised when doing my exams and I can still recall entire speeches to this day. I used this talent to great effect in Latin exams. I loved Latin. My grandfather had also studied it and encouraged me. My Latin primer was signed by Anthony Wedgwood Benn (Tony Benn) who had used it when he was a boy – obviously, we had inherited some great books from Westminster School in London.

I loved the structure, discipline and beauty of the language and still do. I loved Virgil and Ovid and even Caesar's Gallic Wars. I found the fact that this wonderful literature had survived the centuries amazing. It was not a popular subject in the sixties and I found I was the only student at the convent doing it for A level, but I didn't mind at all – I had a fantastic teacher, dear Sister Dominic (who I named my son after), all to myself.

I was encouraged to audition for the famous East Ham Girls' Choir and got in. It was fabulous – they performed all over London and I learned so much beautiful music.

I loved writing as well as reading, any kind and especially poetry. I had two pen pals in the USA, Sherry in Lansing, Michigan and Vinny in Brooklyn, New York. They kept me up to date with music and fashion and America was then still the leader in both, but things were about to change.

6

The Sixties

1965 Zeitgeist

The sixties was the most fantastic time to be young, especially in London.

For the first time, young people had their own identity, fashion and music.

We could get Saturday jobs! At 15, I was delighted to get a job helping out at Boots the Chemist in Forest Gate. I worked from 8:30 a.m. to 6 p.m. for 10 shillings and sixpence and that was my pocket money. It felt like a fortune – enough to buy a top for myself – red and white stripes which I wore with white jeans – the height of fashion! It was the age of Mods and Rockers. This was a sort of gang-culture of the time, a throw-back to the teddy boys and greasers of the 1950s, but really rather tame in comparison. The Mods (boys and girls) had longish hair, usually cut in a neat bob, had their own type of music and rode motor-scooters. The boys wore parkas and the older ones sometimes dressed up in shot-silk mohair suits for dances. The girls wore crisp gingham shirts and white jeans or short skirts with white sneakers. The Rockers were exactly that – loud, long haired and rode motorbikes – we also called them "greasers". They wore jeans and t-shirts with leather jackets. They liked loud rock music and I thought they were a bit rough and dangerous. They always seemed to be around when there was any sort of trouble and there were frequent "wars" between both factions, usually at seaside resorts like Eastbourne or Brighton on Bank Holidays! We were discouraged from attending any sort of gathering for fear of getting involved. My parents' mantra was "show me your friends and I'll show you what you are" – and we did what we were told!

Although I was neither a Mod nor a Rocker, being rather too young at 15, I did hanker after the Mod fashion. My waist-long hair was cut into a shorter bob with a fringe. I went to concerts all over London with my sister, who had left school and now worked for FilmFair, a film and tv production company in London. She suddenly had become a very sophisticated "dolly bird" and I was more than happy to tag along.

7
Ready Steady Go!

There was a tv show called Ready Steady Go! on London Weekend Television.

It was fronted by Cathy McGowan, a young London girl with the Mod "look".

Cathy is now the partner of Michael Ball. I saw an article in the paper that they were looking for youngsters to be audience members on the show, which was broadcast live every Friday at 6 p.m. I resolved to have my hair cut just like Cathy's and I was determined to get on the show.

In June 1965, I queued up with hundreds of other young hopefuls at Kingsway in London and lied about my age. I said I was 16 and got in.

My audition picture and pass shows me with long hair and still in my school uniform! I was accepted as a "regular" on the show, but had to bunk off school early on Fridays to get to Kingsway (Holborn) in time for the live show. Later, it was broadcast from Wembley.

This was black and white TV and I soon realised everyone wanted to stand out on screen. I made sure I wore conspicuous clothes each week – a white T-shirt with a large Y sewn on it one week, a big hat another week, sunglasses etc and quickly learned where to position myself for the best chance of being caught on camera! The studio was tiny and crowded, so you had to be careful of cameras and cables, whilst all the time watching for where the next artists were being set up to perform. It was just brilliant. I saw all the big music names of the time, met many of them and got tons of autographs. I became quite a celebrity at school, as this was the programme everyone watched and my friends loved it if they spotted me wearing something of theirs, so I was given hats and scarves and even jewellery! If any of the nuns saw the show, they never mentioned it.

Dave Clark (of The Dave Clark Five) bought the recordings of the shows and they are not available to buy, but some survive on YouTube now and if you look very, very closely, you might spot a very young and trendy Carole! Now thinking back, it was all just amazing. I love seeing and hearing these old acts nowadays, the soundtrack of my life in the sixties. I love hearing the music now – and especially seeing the acts perform onstage live after all these years. Although our children have never heard of them and couldn't understand my delight, Chris Farlowe and Georgie Fame actually appeared here in Wiltshire! Many of these great performers are no longer with us, but their music remains. Those that are, are really old!!

Ready Steady Go! – These were just some of the acts I saw during the various series of the show. I was a fan of most, so it was a thrilling experience and a chance to see some of the big American acts live too. There were a few I didn't really care for, including The Rolling Stones, who I thought were just too ugly – although I have always liked their music! LULU (who was the same age as me at the time!)

This certifies that the holder is a

READY STEADY GOER!

Transmission is from WEMBLEY STUDIOS at 6.08 pm on FRIDAYS
The doors open at 5.30 pm and close at 5.50 pm

NAME............Carol Payne............
ADDRESS...........56 Henderson Road............
Forest Gate
E.7.
Date of Birth 17.5.47 ....Phone (if any)................

This card is ONLY evidence that the holder is on the list of dancers for Ready Steady Go
IT MUST BE SHOWN ON REQUEST AND DOES NOT PERMIT ENTRY TO
THE STUDIOS WITHOUT A TICKET. THIS CARD IS STRICTLY NON-
TRANSFERABLE AND MAY BE WITHDRAWN OR CANCELLED WITHOUT
EXPLANATION OR COMPENSATION.   Unit Manager, RSG

THE BEATLES
CILLA BLACK
THE ROLLING STONES
DAVE CLARK FIVE
MANFRED MANN (who performed the show's theme song "5 4 3 2 1")
THE WHO
GEORGIE FAME & THE BLUE FLAMES
THE ANIMALS
THE YARDBIRDS
THE ZOMBIES
DUSTY SPRINGFIELD

HERMAN'S HERMITS (the lead singer, Peter Noone, signed his name on my arm, which I displayed proudly at school until it eventually washed off!)
THE KINKS
THE FORTUNES
THE FOURMOST
HELEN SHAPIRO
THEM
SANDIE SHAW
DONOVAN
GERRY & THE PACEMAKERS
FREDDIE & THE DREAMERS
STEVE WINWOOD
CHRIS FARLOWE
SWINGIN' BLUE JEANS
THE BEACH BOYS
THE WALKER BROTHERS
JERRY LEE LEWIS
MARVIN GAYE
THE SUPREMES
ROY ORBISON

BURT BACHARACH
PJ PROBY
BOB DYLAN

SONNY & CHER – one of the very first acts I saw and oh how I loved them!

GENE PITNEY
JIMI HENDRIX
MARTHA & THE VANDELLAS
BILLY J KRAMER & THE DAKOTAS
SMALL FACES

On the show, I mimed as a lookalike to Cilla Black's "You're My World" and Sandie Shaw's "Always Something There to Remind Me" – complete with bare feet!

8

Back to Reality – O Levels

While all the Swinging Sixties was happening, I still had to concentrate on school. I had a large circle of friends and although I was at a girls' school, there were quite a few brothers around so our circle was mixed. My best friends were probably Cecilia (her brother Mark was my first "boyfriend"), Margaret and Sheelagh. Most of the boys attended our partner school, St Bonaventure's. Sixth formers had weekly dance lessons with the boys, which was both embarrassing and sometimes excruciating, but we were all going through the same exam pressures together anyway. St Bonaventure's also had a great music tradition and presented a Gilbert & Sullivan operetta each year, with the younger boys taking the girls' parts. My brother Gordon made a gorgeous Major-General's daughter resplendent in chestnut ringlets in Pirates of Penzance. This started another lifelong passion for G&S and later I performed in several productions myself, eventually directing them.

We spent weekends when we were not working or studying, playing music and singing at each other's houses, which we called "soirees", going to dances or the cinema. Radio was really popular. We had a little Dansette transistor radio and played it all the time, even in bed, learning the words of the songs and listing the top 20 as we listened. Radio Luxembourg, which played all the pop music, gave way to pirate radio, Radio Caroline.

In my house, schoolwork came first and I worked hard. I enjoyed all my lessons except for Maths and History, because a) I wasn't very good at Maths until I suddenly clicked with calculus in my last year and b) We had a really dull History teacher, although I did well and love it now.

I achieved good grades in all seven subjects, even Maths and History, with As in English, Latin, French and, surprisingly, Biology. My headteacher, Mother Mark, wrote on my notification slip (results were sent out by post) "Well done, Carole! Now don't be tempted to rest on your laurels!" I think she knew then I was already getting distracted!

9
1966

The summer of 1966 was amazing and my sister and I were having a great time. Kris was always going out with her friends from work and Chelsea Arts College and keeping me up to date with gossip and fashion. She had met a young American serviceman from the USAF base at Lakenheath, Suffolk. This was John J Mitchell Jr (great name!!), whom she was to marry in 1970. He was very keen to make a good impression on the family and also extremely useful in getting me records of my favourite American groups like The Beach Boys and The Byrds. Kris got us into clubs like the 100 Club, The Flamingo Club, Scott's of St James's and Whisky A Go-Go in London's Wardour Street. It was the place to be seen. My Auntie Pat made me mini-skirts to my own designs and I wore them with patterned tights and long boots and hats.

By now, we had moved to a smaller house in Henderson Road – there was a house opposite where a young band practised most nights. They were to become the Small Faces, one of the biggest and best-known of the time. Ronnie Lane lived in Romford Road, just around the corner.

The Upper Cut Club in Woodgrange Road, owned by boxer Billy Walker (The Blond Bomber) and his brother George, was opened by The Who. The Small Faces became the house band there for some time. The legend Jimi Hendrix wrote Purple Haze at that club.

We knew money was still tight and our parents couldn't afford to keep the house. It was sold and I was very sad to leave the garden. We moved to a rented flat above a hairdresser in Green Street, near the West Ham Football Ground in Boleyn Road.

When we (West Ham) won the Cup in 1966, the whole street, the whole neighbourhood erupted. I and everyone else followed the open-top team bus down Green Street from the Boleyn Ground, screaming at Bobby Moore and Geoff Hurst as if they were pop stars!

At school, I and some friends were involved in voluntary work helping at the London Hospital. We started a little singing group, entertaining old people as well as those in hospital. We sang everything from Christmas Carols to Old Time Music Hall and pop songs, often dressing up to make a bit of a show for them.

There was little careers advice in those days. Our school stressed the importance of following a vocation. This might be the religious life, which, if you were called to it, must NEVER be ignored, or a profession such as teaching or nursing. Whilst several of my schoolfriends may have considered it, I certainly did NOT have a religious vocation. I had always said I wanted to travel – I had never travelled beyond France. I decided to try for University – and I would be the first in our family to do so. I had no idea what I would study or what I would do afterwards. I selected my "A" level subjects – English, French and Latin, with additional "O" levels in Business Studies, French Literature and Greek Literature just because I liked them. I ploughed through loads of different prospectuses, visited Cambridge University and fell in love with it, even though I was too late to do the entrance exam. I dutifully sent off my UCAS application with no real belief that I would be able to go. In my heart I knew my parents were struggling and could not really afford for me not to be working and contributing to the family income.

10

1967 Teenager of the Year

My grandfather was very proud of all of us and was particularly delighted with my "O" level results. He encouraged me to try for university anyway and suggested I should consider a career in the Diplomatic Service, which I might be able to apply for before university. He entered me into the London Evening News Teenager of the Year competition. It was a very big deal. I was shortlisted and invited to an interview. Daddy took me to the Town Hall on his way to his night shift at Ford's, kissed me and wished me luck. Mummy told me not to wake her if I came in late and only to do so if I had good news. There was no merit in coming second, ever. There were several other competitors. We were interviewed separately by a panel, asked about our hobbies and ambitions and I found myself really enjoying it. Two finalists were selected from Newham, one boy and one girl – me!

I crept into the house that night and woke my mother!

For the final, we had to write an essay (1000 words, handwritten) on what the younger generation could offer the world. Sadly, I didn't get any further in the competition, but it was an amazing experience and I loved all the celebrity status that came with it – including a shield and plaque with my name on it. Grandfather Woodhouse was delighted and years later I found he had kept all the newspaper cuttings, now yellowed with age.

In August, my baby brother Keith was born. That made eight of us altogether in the flat. I was 17, it was a big gap and I adored my little brother, but we really needed more space. My parents reluctantly applied to Newham Council for a council house and we went on a waiting list. It was going to be a long and very unsettling experience. My parents had high expectations – too high, really and considered council tenants as beneath them. We were told a brand-new development was being built at Tower Hamlets and we would be homed really quickly. In the event, my parents refused the first two offers, which was a big mistake, because you only got three chances and then you were removed from the waiting list.

Chris – My Knight in Shining Armour!

One day in October 1967, my whole life changed. One of my schoolfriends, Margaret, invited me to her 18th birthday celebration. Her parents had booked her tickets for a film and dinner in London with her boyfriend and another couple. Her boyfriend, Graham, was a medical student at University College Hospital in London and his best friend, Chris, was studying at the Royal Veterinary College. They asked us separately to make up the foursome. I cautiously agreed to go on my first (and only) blind date. It was a warm October afternoon and I wore a floaty pink mini-dress and thought I looked very trendy indeed. I went by bus to Margaret's house in Wanstead, where we were to meet Graham and Chris. I walked in and was greeted by a tall, blue-eyed handsome young man with floppy brown hair and a big smile. I was delighted when he introduced himself as Chris! He was in his second year at University and seemed very sophisticated to me.

Chris, 1967

We all went off to London on the tube and never stopped talking the whole time. We saw Doctor Zhivago on wide screen in Leicester Square and the music, Lara's Theme ("Somewhere My Love"), became our song. It was a fantastic film, VERY long and being set in Russia, there was an awful lot of snow and ice on screen. The cinema had air-conditioning and it was so realistic we were freezing! Chris very gallantly gave me his jacket to put over my shoulders. We had dinner at The White Bear Inn – steak and red wine – a first for me. I was only 17 and still at school and although we knew we were meant to be together, Chris had to finish his degree and my parents were very strict about not going out on school nights. We didn't have a phone, so we kept in touch by letter – and in those days, the post came twice a day! Chris sent me a letter the day after we met inviting me to a formal dinner out with his parents that same week. From then on life was a complete whirl.

We both loved music of all kinds and Chris played guitar really well. We went to folk clubs and he persuaded me to sing along with him. I was very nervous at first, but with his encouragement my confidence grew and we became quite popular as a duo! We covered lots of folk music, Peter Paul and Mary, Pete Seeger, Bob Dylan and later, our favourites, Simon and Garfunkel. Chris had actually seen Paul Simon years before in a folk club in Essex and Art Garfunkel was there too, before they formed as a duo called Tom and Jerry!

As students, we had little money to spare and often went to a pub in Stratford called "The Two Puddings" where they had live music. Half a pint of cider could last quite a long time! Much, much later to our delight, we discovered Harry and Sandra Redknapp went to the same pub when they were courting.

We took advantage of heavily discounted theatre tickets and nightclub passes, including Oh! What a Lovely War directed by the legendary Joan Littlewood at the Theatre Workshop in Stratford. We saw Sir John Gielgud in Forty Years On, while we sat way up in the gods. We saw John Mayall and Cream and saved for tickets to the rock musical HAIR! at the Shaftesbury Theatre – 12 shillings each! On stage in that production were a very young Paul Nicholas and Elaine Paige (nude!).

Audience tickets for our favourite "Country Meets Folk" weekly radio show recorded at The Playhouse Theatre at Charing Cross were free and Chris's lovely parents were always taking us out to dinners and shows. They also invited me to come on conference trips and masonic banquets with them which was great fun as these often-included formal black-tie events at very smart venues like The Dorchester, The Ritz and Café Royal!

Me with Mum and Dad Berry outside "Glenthorne", their house in Shenfield, Essex 1968.

Chris could drive and often found himself driving us in his parents' beautiful Daimler to parties and dances. It was fantastic and I felt like a princess in it.

I started a scrapbook and keepsake box of programmes and tickets, cards and letters collected over the years, which soon got completely out of hand as I'm such a hoarder, but so useful for compiling these memoirs!

11
1968

In June 1968, I took my A levels. Many of my friends had also applied to university and we eagerly awaited the results. I had an interview at Queen Mary College, London to study French, but the professor who was to interview me was late due to fog and in a terrible mood and I was nervous so it didn't go well. I wasn't very impressed anyway. I had offers from Royal Holloway and Exeter too, all three to do different courses. When the results came, I still had no idea what I should do. If I decided to accept a university place, that would delay our wedding and I didn't know where Chris would be working either. My parents really needed me to contribute to the family income, so I decided to apply for some jobs during the summer.

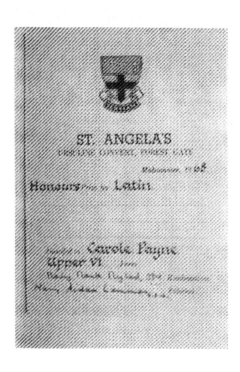

ST. ANGELA'S
URSULINE CONVENT, FOREST GATE

Honours in Latin

Carole Payne
Upper VI

We had decided very early on that we would get married. Chris had told his next-door neighbours, Pat and David, that I was "the one" soon after we met. Pat and David were very fond of Chris and became our closest friends. We spent almost as much time in their house as we did in Mum and Dad's. They had a friend called Humphrey who was a graphologist. He analysed our handwriting and declared that we would have "a very long, exciting and happy life together, with many adventures".

Chris chose my ring, exactly what I wanted: an elegant solitaire diamond in a square setting and we got officially engaged at a Masonic Dinner with Chris's parents a year to the day after we first met. Both sets of parents felt we were too young, so we agreed to wait until Chris could get a job before we got married. I started a "bottom drawer" under the direction of my grandmother. This was a tradition – to store things a young bride would need for her wedding and first home and included my trousseau, linen (I even embroidered our pillowcases!), towels, basic cooking utensils and gadgets, cookery books and ornaments – nice, but not all very useful. My grandmother's first contribution to start me off was a pair of exquisite, delicate and completely impractical white kid gloves!

My parents had to accept the final housing offer or lose the chance of a council house completely and we moved again – to a flat in a decidedly dodgy-looking tenement in Whitechapel. There was quite a stir when Mr Berry's Daimler or chauffeur-driven limousine came to pick me up for a function. It's now a very desirable place to live, but at the time it didn't seem very nice at all.

It was, however, a quite interesting place to live! The Brady Street Jewish Cemetery is located a few hundred yards from Whitechapel Road. The cemetery reached maximum capacity in 1858. One famous occupant is Nathan Mayer Rothschild, one of the founders of the banking dynasty and once the wealthiest man on earth.

Durward Street, formerly Bucks Row, is a road off Brady Street, where Jack the Ripper victim Mary Ann Nichols was murdered on 31st August 1888.

Opposite the Collingwood Estate where we lived were the Brady Street Mansions – tall and imposing Edwardian buildings where one could see the beautiful chandeliers inside lit up at night. This was such a contrast to the drab council homes.

A youth gang known as the Brady Street Massive is known to operate in this area now and are linked to the local drug trade, kidnapping and extortion.

It was a notorious area for criminal activity going back years to Jack the Ripper.

People remembered the famous Kray Twins with affection, the Blind Beggar Pub was on the corner and it was often said London had never been safer (especially for women) than when the Krays were looking after it. Our neighbours were rough and noisy and it was normal for Police sirens to be heard at all hours, but people were friendly and looked out for one another. It was also very easy to get to work as it was so near to the City. I soon realised it really was safe for a young woman to walk home from Whitechapel tube station on her own, although my father still insisted on meeting me to walk me home if it was dark.

The Blind Beggar, Whitechapel Road

I applied for a job at Commercial Union Assurance in Cheapside as a trainee. This was a very easy commute from Whitechapel. It meant I could do a day release course in Business Studies, Banking and Insurance at City of London College (now City University) while earning money. The job was boring, but I stuck with it and it was fantastic working and living in London.

With Chris, I was enjoying the social side of university without actually having to do any studying. I went to all the clubs and shows with him while he was in residence at International Hall. The LSE was just around the corner too and they had some amazing gigs. We saw Queen and Status Quo while they were relatively new on the scene and playing Student Union bars, as well as countless plays and shows at student discount prices.

I needed to start saving if we were to get married as soon as Chris qualified – in three years' time. I got a part-time evening job at I Was Lord Kitchener's Valet, a trendy boutique in Piccadilly Circus. This was really fun and not too far from where Chris was staying in halls. All sorts of people came into the boutique late at night and I enjoyed the celebrity spotting very much indeed. One evening as I waited at the bus stop for the No 25-bus home, I found myself chatting to a very young dancer who was appearing with Keith Michel in Man of La Mancha. It turned out to be Wayne Sleep.

I even managed to blag a part-time job for a short time as a house model! This was at a fashion house in Commercial Road, Rensor, which produced the most exquisite tailoring for women. I loved it.

Chris had his own car – a much-loved and cared-for little red Austin A40 with the very apt number plate for a vet – 508 MOO. We went everywhere in it and even took it on the ferry to Ireland. Our parents were quite nervous about us going away on our own – especially camping! It was going to be very basic, but Mum and Dad Berry made sure we were well equipped with air beds, sleeping bags and cooking stove and utensils. We took the ferry from Fishguard and I was sick the whole way, of course. I really did not enjoy sea travel any more than my mother did.

Once we arrived in Ireland, we set off with our maps and headed down to Cork, intending to follow the coast as far as we could west, then across the country back to Dublin. It was our first adventure and so much fun, though not without mishaps. The air beds Dad Berry had so carefully selected, began to deflate after the very first night, so we slept on the hard ground for the entire 18 days. We camped freely anywhere, cooking outside on our little stove with Chris playing his guitar by the light of a proper campfire. We had a little ridge tent, just big enough for the two of us. One night the weather was particularly rough and Chris had to hold the tent up on the inside while the winds roared and howled like banshees. Another night, we decided to drive to small town where a "dance" was advertised. It was a scary ride along very narrow, mountain roads in the dead of night. When we got there, we found the hall was empty, although clearly set up for a dance. This was Ireland, of course. A local told us everyone was in the pub and would head for the dance as soon as the pub closed – they did and it was a hoot! Everyone joined in and we danced and laughed all evening, then had to face the drive back, only to find part of the road had disappeared during the night and we had to take a detour! Our car seemed very popular – people waved and smiled as we passed – it was only later we realised this was their usual way of hitch-hiking!

Ireland was wonderful. We promised ourselves we would return and we did.

Once I'd finished my ACII (Associate of the Chartered Institute of Insurers) course, I knew my future was never going to be in insurance. I saw an ad for a job at The Times Newspapers selling classified advertising. It was fabulous. We had a wonderful week of induction, seeing how the paper was put together and produced in those days, with manual typesetters and proper proof-readers. I was fascinated by the process. We were introduced to William Rees-Mogg (father of Jacob!), the editor.

Being a tele-ad girl was fantastic. The job was at Printing House Square, off Fleet Street, a wonderful and historic part of London. The sales team were great, dynamic and a lot of fun. I was good at selling too and I could use my creative talents in writing advertising copy. I learned to type on an electric typewriter and completed my diploma in Business Studies.

1969 and my skirts were getting shorter. I entered a couple of local beauty contests including Miss Newham and Miss

Wavy Line (!). I didn't win, but enjoyed myself immensely and I was spotted as a "poster girl" for The Times Literary Supplement. I soon progressed to having responsibility for advertising in the Epicure section of the daily newspaper, which involved calling and visiting some of the best restaurants, food and wine suppliers in town. This had its advantages, including discounted dinners and many gifts of wine.

Lulu married Maurice Gibb of the Bee Gees in February and in March Paul McCartney of The Beatles married Linda Eastman and John Lennon of The Beatles married Yoko Ono!

Babbacombe 1969

We continued to spend lovely holidays in Devon, which became our favourite place, with Chris's parents and the weather was always fine! Chris' brother Peter and his wife also invited us to spend lovely weekends at the house they were building (complete with swimming pool) in Hampshire.

12
July 1969

It was an exciting time globally too. Chris and I sat up all night to watch Apollo 11 land on the moon.

From The Times, I was eventually headhunted for another (much better paid) job at an insurance brokers' office (Towry Law) in London Wall. My boss there was Sir Clive Scott Hopkins, a very charismatic and brilliant financier who never seemed to stop working. We were all in awe of him, but he worked so hard, I wondered if that sort of stress was worth it.

My insurance course did actually pay off eventually, although it was never going to be my career, because we got married in May 1971, the year of decimalisation, a week before my 21st birthday.

13

Married Life

1971 was a good year – the best of my life up until then. Chris qualified as a veterinary surgeon in April – BVetMed MRCVS. and started applying for jobs. We wanted to get married as soon as possible, so arranged the wedding in Forest Gate the next month, at the church of my childhood. Chris had to take weekly instruction in the Catholic faith and to agree to bring up our children as Catholics, which he duly did.

In those days, vets usually lived in practice accommodation, which was good for us, because we had no money for a house anyway. Chris's first job was to be in Huntingdon, in Cambridgeshire. It was a mixed practice (small and large animal) with three partners. The practice arranged for us to live in a nice little house, which Chris had to furnish and get ready for me to come to immediately after our honeymoon. He had just four weeks.

The Wedding

Our wedding on 8th May 1971 was a simple but beautiful affair at St Antony's Church. It was a glorious warm sunny day. It wasn't without its mishaps, however. The wedding before ours, booked for 3:30 p.m. was late, so ours was delayed. We had a beautiful black and burgundy Daimler car to take me to the church. My driver had to keep driving around the block until we could go in! Poor Chris was left sweltering outside the church.

Chris's older brother Peter was Best Man and my little sister Berni was my bridesmaid. My flowers were simple balls of blossom hanging from ribbons, mine white roses with lily of the valley (my favourites) and Berni's were yellow roses to match her dress. The buttonholes were traditional white roses and carnations. My old head teacher Mr Mangham from my primary school was the Deacon. 50 guests, including my old school friends, joined us for a meal in The Adelphi Rooms, Stratford. Another friend from our circle, Peter Crush, acted as DJ.

We then had a mad dash to get to Paddington Station for our train to Devon. We took a picnic from the reception as we had had no time to eat, with a bottle of champagne for the journey! We jumped into our reserved seats in our carriage and settled down for the long train journey. A man also got into our carriage, took one look at us clutching our champagne and covered in confetti, congratulated us formally, then bowed and left us alone – how chivalrous, we thought!

Our official photographer had problems with his camera. No digital images in those days, sadly. Consequently, our pictures are far from perfect, with double images and bad colour fixing. We have some taken by guests too, so we do have our memories of a lovely day!

We spent a magical week at Danby Lodge, in Babbacombe, Devon, which was the first place Mum and Dad Berry had taken me to on holiday. The owners, Ted and Marion, gave us the whole week as a wedding gift. And we were the only guests, the weather was brilliant, so it was just wonderful.

After our idyllic honeymoon, we came back to London, collected my limited belongings, including my cards, gifts and scrapbook and the remains of our wedding cake, from the flat in Whitechapel, then went straight to Huntingdon to start our next adventures together. Suddenly it was just the two of us and our whole lives ahead of us.

There would be so many more stories to tell.

Chris's work and our busy lives would take us from Cambridgeshire to Wales, Essex, Berkshire and Wiltshire, with some surprising events along the way. We would have a family of our own and I would have several different occupations and I would travel!

The family was scattered all over the world and we were to visit them on wonderful holidays through the years. My Uncle Mickey and Auntie Jean had gone to Canada and founded a new Woodhouse family there. My sister Kristin had gone to live with her new husband in Louisville, Kentucky. My brother Gordon went to Australia soon after our wedding, closely followed by younger brother Ian. Chris's sister Janice had already gone to Australia and started a new life there. My youngest sister Bernadette went to live in the Middle East, Far East and finally Houston, Texas. Baby brother Keith, working at British Airways, travelled all over the world and lived in South Africa and Germany, before finally settling in London. We have all come a very long way.